SCHOOL PUBLISHERS

Photos:
p. 2, fox © Harcourt Telescope; p. 4, six © Harcourt Telescope; p. 8, Max © Corbis; p. 3, © Shutterstock;
p. 5, © Shutterstock; p. 6, © Harcourt Telescope; p. 7, © Harcourt Telescope.

Printed in China

ISBN 10: 0-15-358377-0
ISBN 13: 978-0-15-358377-3

Ordering Options
ISBN 10: 0-15-358355-X (Grade K Below-Level Collection)
ISBN 13: 978-0-15-358355-1 (Grade K Below-Level Collection)
ISBN 10: 0-15-360630-4 (package of 5)
ISBN 13: 978-0-15-360630-4 (package of 5)

4 5 6 7 8 9 10 0940 15 14 13 12 11 10 09

fox

box

six

OX

mix

fix

Max